D0810487

CAREERS FOR
HEROES

AIR
MARSHALS

Kate Rogers

PowerKiDS
press.

New York

Published in 2016 by The Rosen Publishing Group, Inc.
29 East 21st Street, New York, NY 10010

First Edition

Editor: Katie Kawa
Book Design: Mickey Harmon

Photo Credits: Cover (woman) Monkey Business Images/Shutterstock.com; cover (background) egd/Shutterstock.com; cover, p. 5 (emblem) https:// upload.wikimedia.org/wikipedia/commons/thumb/b/bf/U.S._Federal_Air_Marshal_ Service_patch.jpg/200px-U.S._Federal_Air_Marshal_Service_patch.jpg; cover, pp. 1, 3, 4, 6, 8, 10, 12, 14, 16, 18, 20–24 (gray and yellow textures) siro46/ Shutterstock.com; p. 5 (main) Pavel L Photo and Video/Shutterstock.com; p. 7 (main) Joseph Sohm/Shutterstock.com; p. 7 (inset) https://commons.wikimedia.org/wiki/ File:John_F._Kennedy,_White_House_color_photo_portrait.jpg; p. 9 Andresr/ Shutterstock.com; p. 11 (main) IM_photo/Shutterstock.com; p. 11 (inset) michaeljung/ Shutterstock.com; p. 13 (main) John Roman Images/Shutterstock.com; p. 13 (inset) bikeriderlondon/Shutterstock.com; p. 15 kilukilu/Shutterstock.com; p. 17 (top) https://commons.wikimedia.org/wiki/File:CGIS_Firearms_Training.jpg; p. 17 (bottom) Joe Raedle/Getty Images News/Getty Images; p. 19 (inset) John Wollwerth/ Shutterstock.com; p. 19 (main) Vetal/Shutterstock.com; p. 22 (man) Hugo Felix/ Shutterstock.com; p. 22 (plane) Ivan Cholakov/Shutterstock.com.

Library of Congress Cataloging-in-Publication Data

Rogers, Kate, author.
 Air marshals / Kate Rogers.
    pages cm. — (Careers for heroes)
 Includes index.
 ISBN 978-1-5081-4387-1 (pbk.)
 ISBN 978-1-5081-4388-8 (6 pack)
 ISBN 978-1-5081-4389-5 (library binding)
 1. United States. Federal Air Marshal Service—Juvenile literature. 2. Sky marshals—United States—Juvenile literature. 3. Airlines—Security measures—United States—Juvenile literature. 4. Law enforcement—Vocational guidance—United States—Juvenile literature. I. Title.
 HV8144.F37R64 2016
 363.28'7602373—dc23
                                    2015029569

Manufactured in the United States of America

CPSIA Compliance Information: Batch #BW16PK: For Further Information contact Rosen Publishing, New York, New York at 1-800-237-9932

CONTENTS

SAFETY IN THE SKY

Different kinds of police officers and other heroes keep us safe on the ground, but who keeps us safe in the sky? Air marshals are special law **enforcement** officials whose job is to keep people safe on airplanes and in airports. They work as part of a United States government program called the Federal Air Marshal Service (FAMS).

Air marshals are trained to recognize the signs of potential, or possible, danger on a flight. They're also trained to handle any **threats** to passengers or crew on an airplane by using force if they feel it's necessary. Air marshals have a very important job!

FAST FACT!

The FAMS is part of the Transportation Security Administration (TSA), which is a part of the U.S. government created to help keep U.S. travelers safe.

An air marshal doesn't travel on every flight. However, someone who wants to harm passengers on a plane can't count on being able to tell which flights have an air marshal. Air marshals don't wear uniforms. They dress like ordinary passengers. Almost any adult passenger on any flight could be an air marshal!

THE HISTORY OF THE FAMS

The FAMS might seem like a relatively new government program, but it's actually been around in different forms for over 50 years! In 1962, 18 people were **deputized** to help prevent hijackings of flights. A hijacking happens when a person or group illegally takes control of a plane and forces it to go to a different place than it was supposed to.

The FAMS greatly increased its ranks after the **terrorist** attacks of September 11, 2001. It grew from under 100 members to the thousands of people who currently work as air marshals all over the United States.

FAST FACT!

The FAMS officially started in 1968. At that time, it was called the Sky Marshal Program.

Ronald Reagan

John F. Kennedy

In the 1960s, President John F. Kennedy was the first to put law enforcement officials on planes. In 1985, President Ronald Reagan increased the number of air marshals in a push to keep the skies safe for travelers.

How do air marshals keep us safe when we fly? They're trained to recognize terrorist **behaviors** in order to spot potential threats. Air marshals need to always be alert in order to continue looking for terrorist behavior. They can't ever sleep on a flight when they're working.

If an air marshal does spot a terrorist or another dangerous, or unsafe, person on a flight, they're trained to fight in close quarters. Air marshals also learn how to restrain, or hold down, a possibly dangerous person to keep them from harming others until the plane safely lands.

FAST FACT!

If an air marshal needs to use their gun, they know how to do so with the highest **accuracy** possible. Air marshals are trained to be some of the most accurate shooters in any area of federal law enforcement.

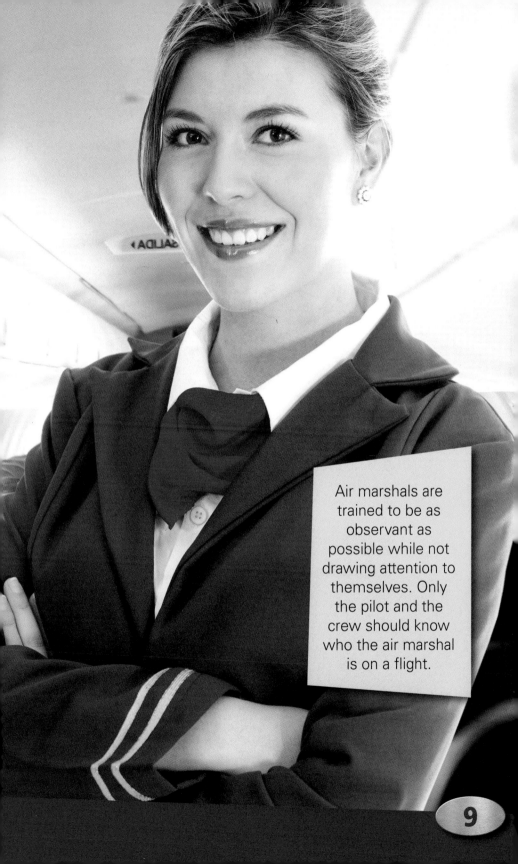

Air marshals are trained to be as observant as possible while not drawing attention to themselves. Only the pilot and the crew should know who the air marshal is on a flight.

BECOMING AN AIR MARSHAL

If you're interested in a career in law enforcement and like to travel by airplane, then you might make a good air marshal. However, it's not easy to get a job with the FAMS. There are many requirements you must meet before you can become an air marshal.

First, you need to go to school. In order to be an air marshal, you should have at least a four-year college degree. You also must be at least 21 years old. In most cases, new air marshals aren't over 37 years old. However, there are some exceptions to that rule.

FAST FACT!

An air marshal must be able to get and keep Top Secret security clearance. This means the U.S. government trusts them with potentially dangerous secret **information**.

Air marshals travel constantly. They need to be ready to travel wherever they're needed, including other countries.

LEARNING FROM EXPERIENCE

Air marshals must have certain skills in order to be good at their job. Work **experience** helps people **develop** those skills before becoming air marshals.

Getting work experience at a job that calls for strong problem-solving skills is a good way to prepare for a career as an air marshal. Air marshals should also be orderly and good at planning, so jobs that call for those skills are good starting points. Finally, **communication** is an important part of an air marshal's job. This includes being able to write well. Gaining experience with these skills is helpful for anyone who wants to be an air marshal.

FAST FACT!

People who think they have what it takes to be an air marshal can apply for the job on a government jobs website.

Serving as a police officer or a member of the military is good work experience for a career as an air marshal.

TESTS AND BACKGROUND CHECKS

After applying for a job as an air marshal, a person is **interviewed** before going through medical tests. They also must pass a physical fitness test. Air marshals must be in good shape in order to do their job well, so this fitness test is very important.

A full background check is also conducted on potential air marshals. Members of the TSA speak to former bosses and even neighbors of people seeking to become air marshals. Air marshals are given access to top-secret national security information, so the TSA must be sure they can be trusted.

FAST FACT!

The fitness test for potential air marshals includes sit-ups, push-ups, pull-ups, and running.

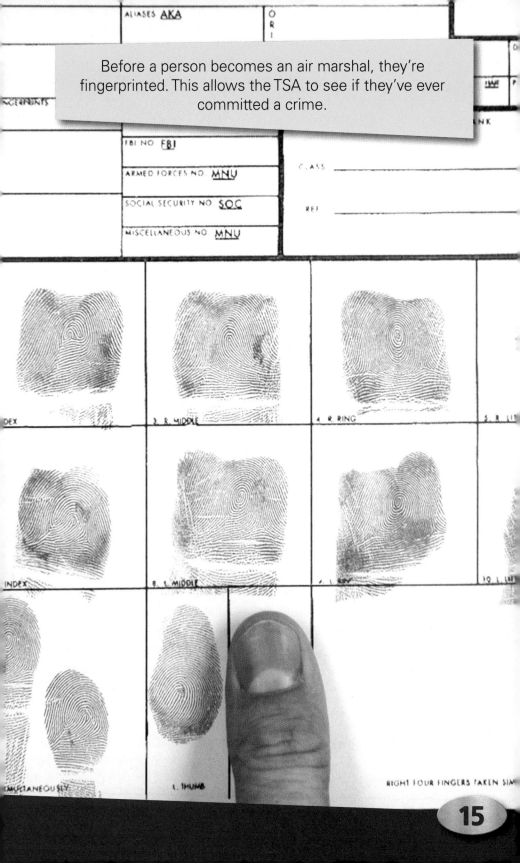

Before a person becomes an air marshal, they're fingerprinted. This allows the TSA to see if they've ever committed a crime.

TWO KINDS OF TRAINING

Before air marshals can start **protecting** people on airplanes, they must first go through weeks of training. The first part of the training occurs in New Mexico. During this time, new air marshals are taught the basics of law enforcement, including basic training in how to accurately shoot a gun.

The next part of air marshal training occurs at the FAMS Training Center in Atlantic City, New Jersey. This training includes specific physical skills used by air marshals, such as fighting in close quarters, restraining a dangerous person, and protecting themselves and others while on the ground.

FAST FACT!

Training with firearms, or guns, is an important part of all air marshal training. Before any training can begin, a new air marshal must show they understand gun safety.

Air marshals go through many different training exercises, such as the ones shown here, before they begin working on airplanes.

NO SMOKING!

Most of the time, air marshals fly from one place to another and never have to use their training. The knowledge that there could be an air marshal on a plane is sometimes enough to keep people from trying to do dangerous things. However, there have been a few cases where air marshals were called upon to protect people on airplanes.

One such example happened on a United Airlines flight in April 2010. After a man stepped out of an airplane bathroom smelling like smoke and wouldn't give up his lighter, air marshals stepped in. They kept the man in his seat until the plane safely landed.

FAST FACT!

If an air marshal believes there's the potential for danger on an airplane, they know to tell the pilot to activate a national alert system to warn all airplanes in flight.

Smoking on planes is illegal, and the man on the United Airlines flight was smoking a pipe in the bathroom. Though there was no real danger on that flight, the air marshals were praised for their quick handling of what could have been a scary set of events.

OTHER FAMS CAREERS

Are you interested in working for the FAMS, but not sure if you want to be an air marshal? Don't worry—the FAMS has many jobs to choose from that all help make our skies safer. Some people who work for the FAMS gather intelligence, or information about threats. Others develop or repair the latest **technology** used to protect people on airplanes.

The FAMS is also always on the lookout for people to teach and train air marshals. If you have a special skill air marshals need to have and like teaching others, this could be a great job for you.

FAST FACT!

FAMS intelligence officers gather important information from places and people within the United States and around the world.

FAMS
career areas

1. **air marshal service**

2. **intelligence**

3. **information technology**

4. **law enforcement training**

5. **nursing**

6. **security**

These are just some of the many career areas open to people who want to work for the FAMS. Do any of these sound like cool careers to you?

QUIET HEROES

Air marshals don't do their job for the glory that sometimes comes with heroic careers. In fact, most people will never know if they were on an airplane with an air marshal. An air marshal's job is to quietly keep us safe while we fly.

While we don't often see air marshals at work, that doesn't mean their job isn't important. They play a huge part in protecting travelers and those who work on airplanes. If you think you have what it takes to be an air marshal, someday you might be one of these heroes in the sky!

GLOSSARY

accuracy: The state of being free from mistakes.

behavior: The way a person acts.

communication: The use of words, sounds, signs, or behaviors to convey ideas, thoughts, and feelings.

deputize: To give someone the power to do something in place of another person.

develop: To cause something to become more advanced.

enforcement: The act of making sure people do what is required by law.

experience: The length of time someone has been doing an activity.

information: Knowledge or facts about something.

interview: A formal meeting to gain information in order to decide if someone is qualified for a job.

protect: To keep safe.

technology: The use of science for practical purposes.

terrorist: A person who uses violence to scare people as a way of achieving a political goal.

threat: Someone or something that could cause harm.

INDEX

WEBSITES

Due to the changing nature of Internet links, PowerKids Press has developed an online list of websites related to the subject of this book. This site is updated regularly. Please use this link to access the list: www.powerkidslinks.com/chero/airm